The Promise

Alexei Arbuzov, Russian dramatist, actor and director, was born in 1908. His work includes *Tanya* (1939), *It Happened in Irkutsk* (1959), *The Promise* (1965), *Tales of Old Arbat* (1970), and *An Old-Fashioned Comedy* (1978).

Nick Dear's theatre credits include *The Art of Success* at the Royal Shakespeare Company and Manhattan Theatre Club, New York. It won him the John Whiting Award for 1986, and he was nominated for Laurence Olivier Awards for both this and *A Family Affair*. Other plays include *The Villains' Opera* (National Theatre, 2000), *Summerfolk* (after Gorky; National Theatre, 1999); *Zenobia* (RSC, 1995); *The Last Days of Don Juan* (after Tirso de Molina; RSC, 1990); *In the Ruins* (Royal Court, 1990); *Food of Love* (Almeida, 1988); *A Family Affair* (after Ostrovsky; Cheek by Jowl, 1988); and *Temptation* (RSC, 1984). He has written the libretti for three operas, *A Family Affair* (1993) and *Siren Song* (1994), both premièred at the Almeida Opera Festival, and *The Palace in the Sky* (ENO/Hackney Empire, 2000). His screenplays include *Persuasion* (1995; BAFTA Award); *The Gambler* (1997); *The Turn of the Screw* (1991); and *Cinderella* (2000). He has also written extensively for radio.

ALEXEI ARBUZOV

The Promise

a new version by
Nick Dear

based on the translation by
Ariadne Nicolaeff

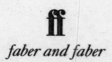

faber and faber

First published in 2002
by Faber and Faber Limited
3 Queen Square London WC1N 3AU
Published in the United States by Faber and Faber Inc.
an affiliate of Farrar, Straus and Giroux LLC, New York

Typeset by Country Setting, Kingsdown, Kent CT14 8ES
Printed in England by Mackays of Chatham plc, Chatham, Kent

A CIP record for this book
is available from the British Library

ISBN 0-571-21595-5

2 4 6 8 10 9 7 5 3 1

The Promise in this version was commissioned by and premièred at the Tricycle Theatre, London, on 25 February 2002. The cast in order of appearance was as follows:

Lika Jenny Jules
Marat Paul Nicholls
Leonidik Gyuri Sarossy

Director Nicolas Kent
Designer Bunny Christie
Lighting Designer Matthew Eagland
Sound Designer Greg Fisher

Characters

Marat

Lika

Leonidik

Act One: March to May 1942
Act Two: March to May 1946
Act Three: December 1959

The action takes place in Leningrad

Act One

SCENE ONE

30 March 1942. One of the few habitable apartments in a semi-derelict house on Fontanka. The room is almost bare; the furniture's been used for firewood. Only a double bed and a large sideboard remain. There is a stove in one corner. It's out. Lika lies on the bed, wrapped in a blanket. It will soon be evening. The door opens slowly and Marat stands on the threshold. He looks around the room in surprise. He sees Lika. She looks at him with frightened eyes.

Lika Who are you?

Marat Well, who are you? (*Pause.*) I mean – what are you doing here?

Lika Living.

Marat How'd you get in?

Lika Caretaker. There were no dead bodies in this room. And the glass was still in the windows. It was a miracle. You won't kick me out, will you?

Marat doesn't answer.

Don't. Please. I've been living here for nearly a month. I've got used to it.

Marat (*looking round the room*) There were some things here . . . some furniture, you know, personal stuff . . . Where is everything?

Lika I burnt it.

Marat All of it?

1

Lika All of it.

Marat sits on the window sill. Pause.

Who are you?

Marat I used to live here. It's our room.

Lika . . . So where have you been?

Marat That's my business. – Listen, there was a photo on the wall, here, between the windows . . . a picture of a naval officer. Have you seen it?

Lika I burnt it.

Marat (*viciously*) Oh, terrific. I hope it kept you nice and warm.

Lika It wasn't the only one. There were loads of photographs; I burnt them all. It was a pretty good fire. Picture frames burn well.

Marat You've made a right mess of the sideboard.

Lika What's wrong with it? It's still there. I only took a few bits off it.

Marat Highly efficient, aren't you? (*quietly*) That was my childhood you burnt.

Lika (*cheerfully*) Oh, I recognise you now! It was you! The boy in the rowing boat, the boy on the bicycle! And in the launch, with the officer . . . I didn't burn them straight away, you know. I had a good look first.

Marat How did I do? Did I burn well?

Lika Why are you making fun of me?

Marat . . . I could cry. Want me to cry?

Lika . . . I'm sorry.

Marat Why are you lying there? Have you given up?

Lika No, I just came in. I wanted to get warm, that's all.

Marat (*laughs*) Well, that's one way of doing it. (*seriously*) Why didn't you burn the sideboard?

Lika Too big. Couldn't move it. Couldn't smash it up.

Marat . . . Are you alone?

Lika Yes, I'm alone.

Marat You're not afraid?

Lika Of course I'm afraid. I'm not stupid. (*Pause.*) It's not so bad when there's gunfire. At least it means someone's *alive* . . . But when there's suddenly a silence . . . then I'm afraid. (*puzzled*) What am I afraid of? No one's going to break in. This building is classed as derelict. The stairs look dangerous. No stranger would risk it. – They're all right, actually, the stairs. Just look bad. On this landing there's only one other apartment with people in it. And they've stopped going out. I bring them their bread ration. In return they said I can have their furniture when they don't . . . need it any more. (*Pause.*)

Marat What about on the next landing? Anyone?

Lika Empty. Friends of yours?

Marat There was a girl who lived there. Lelya. She was supposed to have gone to Tbilisi in the autumn.

Lika She must have, then.

Marat Where did you live?

Lika Number 6, down the road.

Marat I don't remember you.

Lika I was just a little girl before the war.

Marat Number 6. (*remembering*) Well, that was rotten luck.

3

Lika Nothing left.

Marat Was anyone in when – ?

Lika Nanny. My mother's an army doctor, she's at the front. I stayed with Nanny. She was part of the family, been with us for years . . . The building was hit when I went to get our bread. I ran back. But there was nothing left. Only this one was standing. That was on the first of March. It'll be a month, the day after tomorrow.

Marat What about you? Are you weak?

Lika Not too bad, really. I got three parcels from mother in the winter. Soldiers brought them . . . But I suppose there won't be any more parcels. Because they won't know where I am.

Marat They'll find you. You look like a lucky one. (*He says it with distaste.*)

Lika Thanks a lot.

Marat How old are you?

Lika I could be sixteen in a fortnight.

Marat Why only could?

Lika Anything might happen.

Marat Come off it – that's too pessimistic! I'm going to be eighteen next year. And you won't catch me having a nervous breakdown about it. I am definitely going to be eighteen.

Lika When I was little, I used to dream about being sixteen, and all the things I'd do. You know what it's like at the cinema? – 'Under-sixteens not permitted.' All the films worth seeing: 'Under-sixteens not permitted'! It's pathetic. Didn't stop me getting in, naturally –

Marat Naturally.

4

Lika – but it might be a pity not to live till I'm legally allowed to.

Marat You'll make it. Now.

Lika I suppose I will. I've had two lots of food coupons for a whole month! Because Nanny was killed on the first.

Marat Oh, there's nothing like having your family killed on the first of the month, is there?

Lika . . . Why do you say these things?

Marat I have what is technically known as a sense of humour. But I'm not a lucky one, like you. (*He takes two ration cards from his pocket.*) *I've* got two lots of food coupons, see? But only for the thirty-first. Only for tomorrow. Trust my people to die on the wrong day. (*He turns away.*)

Lika Don't cry.

Marat I'm not crying. You can get used to anything, can't you?

Lika (*indicates the ration card*) Your mother?

Marat My sister.

Lika Oh.

Marat (*quietly*) See this button? (*It's on his jacket.*) She sewed it on this morning. (*Pause.*) I went to live with her on Kammeny Island when the Germans invaded. Small house, timber, only a couple of storeys. What the hell did they want to bomb it for? (*Pause.*) Her husband joined the militia, back in August, and she was alone there, bloody fool. I kept saying, 'Let's go home, let's go back to the apartment.' But she wouldn't. 'Suppose Kolenka comes back?' she said. 'No, I must stay on the island.' (*Pause.*) If only she'd listened to me, she'd be sitting here now.

5

Lika But nobody knows, do they? – And your parents? Where are they?

Marat My dad's in the navy. It's five months since I had a letter . . . And now there's nothing left of him. Not a single photo. I wish I'd taken one with me.

He stares at Lika.

Lika I didn't know, did I?

A shell explodes nearby. They both jump slightly, but quickly regain their composure.

Pretty close.

Marat Yup.

Lika Should I go?

Marat Where?

Lika (*cautiously*) You haven't got anywhere to go either.

Marat That's a blindingly skilful deduction.

Lika There used to be a little sofa over there.

Marat (*sarcastically*) Did there really?

Lika I didn't know, did I?

Marat . . . What's your name?

Lika Lidya Vasilyevna. Lika. You?

Marat Marat Yevstigneyev. Known as Marik.

Lika If only we had another mattress . . .

Marat No cause for alarm. It's a good big bed.

Lika You're not suggesting we –

Marat Oh, don't panic, we'll fit. Your feet that end, my feet this end.

Lika We can't do that.

Marat Why not?

Lika Well, you know . . .

Marat What's the problem? You're only a girl.

Lika (*doubtfully*) I suppose . . . (*thinking*) We could saw it in half.

Marat Solid steel frame, you dolt. And we haven't a saw.

Lika Well, we'll sort it out tomorrow.

Marat We'll have a root through the other apartments. Might find something.

Lika People have done that already.

Marat (*perching on the corner of the bed*) Not people like me. We'll be fine.

Lika It's a bit of luck there are two pillows. (*She gives him one.*) But you keep your distance.

Marat Oh, give up, will you?

   They both lie down.

Are you laughing?

Lika (*giggles*) You're breathing.

Marat Of course I'm breathing. Bloody hell.

Lika No more silence . . .

Marat Oh, belt up.

SCENE TWO

4 April. An old mattress has appeared. Marat is asleep on it. Lika is on the bed. A neat pile of firewood in the corner is all that's left of the sideboard. It's just after five in the morning. Distant gunfire. The sound of an air-raid siren.

Lika (*waking up*) Marik! Marik!

Marat (*waking up*) What?

Lika It's an air raid!

Marat Thickhead . . . What's the time?

Lika Just after five.

Marat (*cross*) And you woke me up just because of an air raid?

Lika You've only been here five days. I don't know how you feel about air raids.

Marat Oh, for goodness' sake . . . I hate them.

Lika . . . So what shall we do?

Marat We could go on the roof.

Lika No one's been on duty on the roof for ages.

Marat Why not?

Lika We're derelict. That's how we're classed.

Marat Well, if we're derelict, why the hell did you wake me up?

A landmine explodes close by.

Go down to the basement.

8

Lika I don't want to. I'm warm.

Marat I still haven't the slightest idea why you woke me up.

Lika Oh, stop complaining and go back to sleep.

Marat Fat chance of that now. (*Sighs.*) And I was having such a dream . . . !

Lika What was it?

Marat Sugar-loaf . . . with raisins . . . and honey! Then the music started, and I was kissing a girl I know . . .

Lika I wish I hadn't asked you now.

A landmine explodes close by. Marat gets up.

Marat Right, we're going to the basement.

Lika You're very brave all of a sudden. Not a coward, are you?

Marat Come off it – I spent six months on that roof. Do you know how many incendiaries I threw off that roof?

Lika No, I don't. Was she in your form at school?

Marat Who?

Lika The girl you were kissing?

Marat What's that to you?

Lika The girl from the next landing? Lelya?

Marat Maybe.

Lika I expect she's kissed everyone in Tbilisi by now.

Marat Look, if you don't –

The sound of small-arms fire, not far away.

Damn, it's started.

9

Lika There are loads of empty apartments. You can move out tomorrow. And there's an end to it.

Marat I'm not going anywhere.

Lika Oh aren't you? Why not?

Marat You'll never survive without me.

Lika I'll survive, all right. Like you said: I'm a lucky one.

Marat (*cross*) Why, because you had Mummy's little parcels? Nanny's bread ration? Well that's all over and done with, isn't it? Unless I cop it and you get my coupons! But I wouldn't count on it if I were you, because I'm a lucky one, all right? – I'm just as lucky as you are! As a matter of fact the way you live is disgraceful. You've cut yourself off, backed into a hole, curled up in your lair like an animal!

Lika (*indignant*) What are you talking about?

Marat I've hit the nail on the head, haven't I? You've retreated into yourself, cut yourself off from society! You're a child of the Soviet Union! Do you think that is worthy of you?

Another landmine explodes, even closer than before.

Lika I don't know what you mean, Marik!

Lika bursts into tears. Marik looks out of the window.

Marat Nearly got the bridge. Bastards. – Why are you snivelling?

Lika You treat me like a child! You're stupid! I'm not a child!

Marat Fine, all right, you're a young lady – as if that made a difference! Your way of life is wrong! Don't you see that? Wrong! You think you're aloof, you remove yourself, the people are in struggle against the fascist menace, and you spend your days in bed! Isolation causes starvation, you know!

Lika Gosh, you're good at making up slogans, aren't you?

Marat As a matter of fact, young lady, I've only had half of what you've had to eat, in spite of which my morale remains excellent! And that's because I'm a citizen of Leningrad, and I know my civic duty, and I do it, and yes, more besides!

Lika Now you're showing off.

Marat I am not showing off.

Lika (*wiping her eyes*) Then you're telling lies.

Marat That's different.

Lika You've been telling lies for five days non-stop. Am I right?

Marat Of course.

Lika (*interested*) Why do you tell lies?

Marat It's more fun.

Lika Ah.

Marat (*sternly*) I'm taking you out of your shell. I'm taking you down to the Komsomol Centre, and we're going to find you some work. You should start being useful. You're perfectly fit. It's embarrassing just looking at you. You have to help people who aren't.

Lika I have been helping.

Marat Who? The neighbours? Not enough. Not enough! You have to be of service to others, all the time! Understand?

Lika All right.

Marat You don't sound very convinced.

Lika I said all right!

Marat But you sit and read Turgenev all day! Turgenev! Christ! You burnt the entire library, and kept Turgenev!

Lika I like him!

Marat You like him? All that pointless soul-searching in grand country houses? You like it? It doesn't mobilise anyone!

Lika It mobilises me.

Marat Terrific! In that case we'll go to the Centre today and put your name down.

Lika I said all right, didn't I? (*Pause.*) What are we going to do now?

Marat (*viciously*) Who knows?

Lika Marik . . .

Marat What?

Lika Let's light the stove.

Marat Can't. Got to keep the sideboard.

Lika There's loads of it left . . .

Marat No there isn't.

Lika Perhaps we'll get the furniture from next door . . .?

Marat You should be ashamed! Waiting for people to starve to death, so you can get their furniture!

Lika It's awful . . . It's awful! (*Bursts into tears.*)

   Marat goes and sits next to her.

Marat (*gently*) Hey. That's enough. Come on. You can't do this. I mean, you're always crying.

Lika I never cried when I was alone.

Marat I suppose that's my fault, as usual.

Lika No . . . but don't think . . . don't think I want them to die. That's the last thing I want. I just thought that if . . . then we . . . no, it's awful! (*She cries.*)

Marat You're a silly fool, Lika.

He strokes her hair, tentatively.

Lika (*scared*) What are you doing?

Marat Nothing. Calming you down.

Lika Oh.

Marat You don't want me to?

Lika . . . I don't mind.

Marat Don't cry. The neighbours will go on living, and we'll find some more wood.

Lika Promise?

Marat Absolutely.

Lika Then let's light the fire. (*Whispers, fondly.*) Let's light the fire. It'll soon be spring.

Marat strokes her hair.

(*Smiling*) You hear me, Marik? Light it. (*suddenly anxious*) I think you ought to stop calming me down now.

Marat Fine. (*He snatches his hand away, and jumps off the bed.*)

A landmine explodes in the distance.

Lika They're going away. – Marik, why are you looking at me like that?

SCENE THREE

14 April. Towards evening. Lika is at the table, taking tins of food out of a small packing case. Marat enters. Lika runs towards him.

Lika Marik!

Marat Wait! First item: distribution of presents!

He gives her a red rose made of paper.

Marat Happy birthday! Sixteen! Every cinema manager in town must now kiss your boots!

Lika Where did you get it?

Marat Did a swap. Some stuff I didn't need. And there's more. (*He holds out a small lump of sugar, in the palm of his hand.*) Sugar!

Lika Sugar! Thank you. Now, close your eyes.

He closes his eyes. She takes his hand and leads him to the table.

Open them. Look! Let's celebrate! (*He's silent.*) What is it . . .?

Marat You got a parcel.

Lika Yes! Aren't you glad?

Marat Makes my sugar-lump look a bit meagre.

Lika No, not at all! To show you how much it means to me, I shall eat it right now! (*She puts the sugar in her mouth.*) Mmm, bliss! He's quite a man, this Marat! Let's give him a bite too!

She bites a piece off the sugar, and places it in Marat's mouth. They both suck the sugar slowly, with indescribable pleasure.

Marat (*indicating the parcel*) How did it find you?

Lika It's clever. Look, there's condensed milk . . . stew . . . even jam!

Marat (*salivating*) Jam . . .

Lika And a letter. Mother's well. She's got a medal.

Marat So you're happy.

Lika You'll be happy, too, Marik, you'll see. Please don't be sad. I've got what I wanted: I'm sixteen! Let's have a party at once!

Marat Your mother wrote to you.

Lika Don't spoil it . . .

Marat (*softly*) Fine. Let's have a party.

Lika It's the thing to do, isn't it?

Marat stares at her strangely.

Marat Once upon a time an old, old man lived with his old, old wife, in a little house in . . .

Lika What are you talking about?

Marat You wouldn't understand.

Lika Am I such a silly fool?

Marat No. You aren't a fool. (*seriously*) I could tell you what you are. But I shan't.

Lika Oh, bugger off then! – The kettle's boiling. Open some tins!

A shell explodes close by.

It's started.

Marat Twenty-one gun salute in your honour.

Lika . . . I have to say, I think that's a rotten joke.

Marat Well, today it's me that's a fool. A poor bloody fool. I could tell you why. But I shan't.

Lika That's a relief. Have you opened the stew?

Marat (*opening the tin*) We'll eat half of it. No more. Half. Understand?

Lika Yes, commissar.

> *Lika takes the tin of stew and heats it in a pan on the stove.*

Marat What did you do at the Centre today?

Lika We inspected Number 17, down the road. Went through all the apartments, carted out the bodies. It's funny, I'm not scared of corpses any more. I'm used to them. Is that good?

Marat Yup. Probably.

Lika You're a wise man.

Marat Very wise.

Lika What did you do today, oh wise man?

Marat Worked on the water main. Think how terrific it'll be if we can get the supply back on. Spring's coming, be the first of May in a fortnight. (*thoughtfully*) Do you remember May Day?

Lika Oh, yes! Mother and I were on the rostrum once, watching the parade.

Marat It will be the same again.

> *She looks doubtful.*

(*Stubbornly*) It will be. It will be!

Lika No, it won't be the same . . .

Marat What will it be like, then?

Lika I don't know. Different.

Marat Better?

Lika Perhaps. But definitely different.

Marat I don't want it to be different. I want it to be the same.

Lika Poor Marik . . .

Marat shrugs 'maybe'. Pause.

The smell's driving me mad. Can you smell it?

Marat Absolutely.

They stand at the stove, savouring the aroma of the meat.

Lika Lovely, lovely stew . . .

Marat It looks so beautiful . . .

Lika Come on, let's eat it. Quick!

They leap into action, grabbing plates, Lika spooning the stew from the pan.

Marat Equally, now, equally. No, that's too much for me!

Lika But I get to scrape the pan.

Marat My God, talk about a life of luxury . . .!

They sit at the table and eat in silence. Finally Lika pushes away her plate.

Lika Fantastic. And now . . . the milk! Fetch the glasses! Quick!

Lika pierces the tin of condensed milk as Marat fetches glasses. Lika measures the milk out with a spoon.

Marat One spoonful each.

Lika No, two, today.

Marat All right. One and a half.

Lika And biscuits.

Marat Two each.

Lika Three each. Today.

Marat Look, who's in charge of the supply-line here?

Lika I wouldn't've lived without you. We know that.

Marat (*rising*) Your attention, please! I shall now make a speech, that is, propose a toast, that is, deliver a peroration –

Lika A peroration?

Marat A euology!

Lika (*hooting with laughter*) A euology!

Marat Could you control yourself please? (*raising his glass*) Congratulations, Lika. One year ago I was sixteen. So I know what it's like. So I know what you're going through, et cetera, et cetera. But . . . Be happy, Lika. Little Lika . . . who are you? I could tell you. But I shan't.

Lika Bravo! What an orator!

Marat (*the toast*) Fuck Hitler!

Lika (*raising her glass, bravely*) Fuck Hitler!

Marat And long live Lika!

They chink glasses, and drink.

Now I must kiss your hand.

She looks concerned.

It's the protocol. Now you're grown up.

He takes her hand and kisses it lovingly.

Does that please the young lady?

Lika The great Marat Yevstigneyev kissed my hand. Unforgettable experience.

Marat Have you ever kissed anyone?

Lika . . . Let's get this straight. I love my mother and I'd never do anything to displease her.

Marat You always got full marks for conduct, I expect.

Lika Yes. Didn't you?

Marat Never more than three out of five.

Lika I can't say I'm surprised.

Marat So you haven't ever kissed anyone . . . ?

Lika Well, I did once.

Marat (*astonished*) Really? Why?

Lika Oh, it happens, you know . . . The mistakes of one's youth . . .

Marat (*suddenly sad*) Quite.

Lika Mother writes that I should be evacuated to Moscow. When she finds out that Nanny's dead, and the building doesn't exist any more, well . . . she'll pull some strings, I expect.

Marat . . . You better go, then.

Lika . . . You want me to go?

Pause.

Marat (*old man's voice*) Don't leave me here alone, Lydia Vasilyevna. Have pity on our little ones. Don't go.

Lika Idiot.

Marat Absolutely. You don't know what an idiot I am. I could tell you, of course. But I shan't.

Lika It's dark. Open the door of the stove.

Marat We'll lose the heat.

Lika I don't care. It's my birthday.

Marat opens the stove. The room is filled with its flickering light.

Shall we dance?

Marat There's no music.

Lika We don't need it. We've our own. (*She begins to hum a slow waltz.*) Know this one?

Marat Yes.

They both hum the waltz, and circle slowly around the room, holding each other. Distant gunfire.

Lika Marik . . .

They come to a halt.

It's awful . . . there's so much pain and sorrow . . . and here we are –

Marat (*softly*) It's not our fault.

Again they circle the room, humming. Then they stop. They stand still and say nothing for a long time, their arms around each other.

Lika (*breathless with excitement*) Marik . . . Marik . . .

Marat kisses her on the lips.

My God . . . what's going to happen?

Marat I could tell you. (*Whispers.*) But I shan't.

Lika (*happily*) My poor darling Marat.

The door opens. Leonidik staggers in. He takes a few steps towards the fire and falls heavily. Lika and Marat rush towards him.

Leonidik (*mumbling incoherently*) Firewood . . . got firewood . . .

SCENE FOUR

21 April. A week later. A home-made camp bed has appeared in the room for Leonidik. Marat sits beside him. It's the end of another April day – sunset outside the window. Lika enters the room.

Lika Is he asleep?

Marat Yup. Why are you so late?

Lika I was held up at the Komsomol Centre. Have you fed him?

Marat I heated up the porridge when I got back. He's weird. Terrified of hospitals. Couldn't tell you why. He's something of an eccentric.

Lika An eccentric? What's that?

Marat It means he's peculiar. Damn shame he ate all of your parcel. Still, I think he's recovering.

Lika At first I thought he had pneumonia. But obviously it was only a chill. Because if he'd had pneumonia he'd have died.

Marat Yes. You've got to feel sorry for him. I mean, I've seen stacks of people die. But he's nice.

21

Lika The oddest thing is, he doesn't look like anyone. Everyone looks like someone. Except him.

Marat What about me? Who do I look like?

Lika (*thinks*) You look like everyone all together.

Marat Bully for me!

Lika But you've got to admit, it helps, me being a doctor's daughter. I've cured him in a week. Though you've been terrifically useful.

Marat I'm a terrific person. And I look like everyone all together. Not many people can say that.

Lika I wonder why he's got such a funny name: Leonidik.

Leonidik (*eyes closed*) He also wonders that.

Lika You're not asleep!

Leonidik (*pulling himself up*) It is a funny name, isn't it? Leonidik. Leonidik. (*Laughs.*) Who can ever know what a mother is capable of? (*Pause.*) Is your mother alive, Marat?

Marat No. (*Laughs.*) Well, I've never met her. She might be.

Lika The way you two talk is appalling.

Leonidik Why? Marat's a man who loves his father. Simple.

Lika You're both bonkers.

Leonidik We're not bonkers. It's just that we've seen everything. Everything there is to see, we've seen!

Marat Relax, old chap. Lie down. You're not well enough to get hot and bothered.

Leonidik Leonidik. There's no denying it: the name is hilarious. Now he wants to tell you a story. Well, he ate your food parcel, didn't he? That makes you his nearest and dearest. Instant kith and kin. Just add water. (*fiercely*) And he's got to tell someone what happened. (*Pause.*) I loved my mother. I haven't the language to tell you how much I loved her. But my father, well – busy man, you see, always at work, very popular, very successful. Fair enough, he used to try to talk to me, every Sunday, after lunch – but he had no idea when my birthday was, or what I was doing at school. He died five years ago, when I was twelve. Do you remember, in those days we used to bury people, one by one, and make a big fuss about it? Loads of his friends showed up at the cemetery, and they all said what a remarkable man he was. Well, fair enough. But he died, and I didn't feel any different. Nothing really changed. Except we suddenly had less to eat. My mama meant the world to me. She was always cracking jokes, always cheerful, always kind. We did everything together. Then another man came along. Another man . . . can you grasp the significance of those words? . . . And she just – well – forgot me. Mama forgot me. Can you understand that at all? He was hardly young, and hardly handsome. But he'd sing to her, the whole time, singing to her, soft and low . . . At night they'd dance in the sitting room – just the two of them! Dancing! When the war broke out, he wasn't accepted for the army. No surprise: he was so short-sighted, he couldn't tell a tank from a train. Thankfully he wasn't a complete sissy, and didn't go to pieces during air raids. But then the siege began. And then the famine. I watched them get weaker and weaker. By the beginning of this year, they were both emaciated. Oh, I felt sorry for them, of course, but there were things I couldn't forget . . . still can't . . . (*Pause.*) One day, about a month ago, when neither of them had the strength to get off the bed, I saw her give him part of her bread ration. He didn't notice. He just ate it. She grew thinner and thinner. All right, his eyesight was bad, you could say he didn't spot any difference in the portions. But I did! She died looking at him. My mama. Said her last words to me, of course. Know what they were? 'Leonidik, look after him . . .' (*Pause.*) He'd hardly noticed me before. But now everything changed. He started to tell me about his life, how lost he'd been, how she rescued him. And sometimes he'd sing to me the songs he sang to her. One day he stared at me for a very long time. He said, 'Leonidik, you're just like her. It's extraordinary.' And then he started giving me his bread. Naturally I tried not to take it, but he made such a fuss, and he was so delighted when he got me to eat some. When he smiled, the skin split round his mouth. I should've forgiven him, shouldn't I? I know I should've. But I couldn't! It wasn't until just a few hours before he died that he suddenly seemed to understand. And he asked me to forgive him. (*Pause.*) After he was gone I cried. But I still remembered what he'd done to me. I couldn't forget. Still can't.

Lika (*softly*) But that was real love, do you see? Perfect love.

Leonidik I'm the only person who will never see that.

Marat You are definitely eccentric. Why are you telling us this?

Leonidik He doesn't know. Sometimes he's frightened. But now you know what happened. (*Smiles.*) Maybe he'll feel better.

Lika (*thoughtfully*) A human being must always sacrifice everything for others.

Marat That's not true.

   Pause.

Leonidik Say something, Lika.

Lika . . . I'm just thinking about what you told us.

Marat (*jumping up and clapping his hands*) Right, let's move on! Next item: the future! Leonidik, what do you want to be?

Leonidik (*smiles*) A writer of verse.

Lika You mean a poet?

Leonidik Oh no, that sounds far too pompous. I just mean a writer of verse.

Lika Marik, how about you?

Marat A lion-tamer.

Lika (*surprised*) You're joking!

Marat Watch this.

He places two logs on the floor, and balances a plank on top of them.

What is it?

Leonidik A piece of wood?

Marat It's a bridge! Building bridges, that's what I want to do! That'd be interesting, wouldn't it?

Lika Might be. (*to Leonidik*) Mother always wanted me to be a doctor. So when I was a kid I decided – I'll be a doctor! But not just an ordinary doctor, with a white coat and an old bag, sticking a thermometer into your mouth. No! A research doctor! The first to discover – well, you know what I mean.

Leonidik I do.

Marat (*silly voice*) Got to do what Mummy tells you. Or you'll be a naughty little girl! Naughty, naughty!

Leonidik How'd you like to do us all a favour, and quieten down?

Marat Mummy, Mummy, want my potty!

Lika goes up to Marat.

Lika Are you looking for a punch in the face?

Marat (*put in his place*) Time for bed. (*Lies on his mattress.*) Don't talk too loudly. I've got a lot on tomorrow.

Lika goes back to Leonidik.

Leonidik (*thoughtfully*) It seems to me, the only really hard thing in life is to fully understand your own self.

Lika (*interested*) Is that right?

SCENE FIVE

29 April. An overcast, windy spring day. Lika and Leonidik enter from the street.

Leonidik Tired?

Lika Very tired. (*looking around*) Marat hasn't been in.

Leonidik He'll be back. Did you hear the news today? I think in the Ukraine we're beginning something.

Lika I wish it was here! Our boys need a breakthrough! They'll smash the Germans and raise the siege. Do you know how often I dream of it?

Leonidik (*affectionately*) Get some rest. You've had a hard day.

Lika A sad day. To be more precise. (*Lies on the bed.*) There's one thing that scares me more than anything else. It's that we've got used to everything. The starvation, the bombs, the frozen bodies rising out of melting snow . . . we've got used to it all.

Leonidik That's good. It will help us.

Lika With what?

Leonidik The war.

Lika (*surprised*) Will you go and fight?

Leonidik We'll probably be called up in the autumn. Me and Marat are the same age, you know.

Lika Suppose there is no autumn, ever?

Leonidik Won't make any difference.

Lika (*staring at him*) What's going on in your head?

Leonidik Not a thing. He's an invalid; his brain doesn't work at all. Only the second day that he's been out. He sat on a bench and watched how you cleaned up the courtyard and brought out the dead, and sent them away piled on sledges. (*Pause.*) Are we having the furniture from next door?

Lika I don't want it. We'll manage. (*angrily*) Where's Marat?

Leonidik Yesterday evening they shelled the Centre. Maybe he spent the night with someone.

Lika (*worried*) Who?

Leonidik Well, he's not repairing the water main on his own, is he? He's got friends there. Remember he told us about these incredible Komsomols he'd met – a boy called Yura and a girl called Svetlana?

Lika Svetlana, Svetlana, looks like a banana.

Leonidik (*smiles*) Hey, what's got into you?

Lika Stayed the night with a friend! Huh! I'll bet he did! You don't know Marat – he's an awful liar. He tells a lie a second! One day he brought home a kilo of millet.

27

I asked him, 'Where'd you get that?' He said, 'A little girl fell through a hole in the ice, I fished her out, and her parents gave it to me in thanks.' Later on I discovered that he hadn't saved any little girls at all, but had swapped his fur hat for the grain! And there's more, much more – you'll be appalled!

Leonidik I'm sure I will. But another day – all right?

Lika (*losing her temper*) Why, doesn't Marat interest you?

Leonidik Yes, but not all the time.

Lika You know what you are?

Leonidik What?

Lika You're tight-arsed, you are. – Do you really write verse?

Leonidik (*grins*) I have the odd stab at it.

Lika Read me some.

Leonidik It's bad, Lika. No damn good!

Lika Ah, you're just showing off . . .

Leonidik No, I'm not.

Lika Why do you write it, then?

Leonidik I live in hope. The hope that one day I'll write something good.

Lika (*snorts with laughter*) You're hilarious.

Leonidik Fair enough, but don't give yourself a hernia.

Lika You've got dirt on your face. Little boys, honestly! Here, let me wipe it off . . .

> *She spits on her hanky and wipes his face. Marat enters and sees them.*

What blue eyes you have, as blue as blue!

Marat (*silly voice*) Bluer than blue! And half as true!

Lika Marik!

Marat At your service.

Leonidik (*cheerfully*) Told you he'd be back.

Lika (*alarmed*) What's happened to your arm? You're wounded!

Marat (*casually*) A minor skirmish.

Lika What? What?

Marat It's nothing. Let's move on.

Leonidik Hey, you – don't be rude. She's been worrying about you all day.

Marat Then I'm honoured to have been in the thoughts of such a public-spirited young lady.

Leonidik Nicely put.

Marat Wasn't it?

Lika What are you blabbering about?

Marat We're not blabbering. Not at all. (*sharply*) I took a German parachutist prisoner.

Leonidik Did you?

Marat Wasn't at the waterworks yesterday. We were sent to aid the defence of the Kirov factory. There was a right old do. We were put into the line towards evening, just as the shelling began. Spent the night in the dug-out. Well, I woke up, didn't I, and I thought I'd go on a bit of a recce. I climbed over . . . It was pitch dark, drizzling with rain . . . Suddenly in the gloom I saw a man crawling towards a bombed-out house. I went after him. He fought

29

back with a knife – slashed my arm. But I got him. I disarmed the bastard and handed him over to the soldiers.

Lika (*stroking his bandaged arm*) You're quite a man, Marat.

Leonidik Well done! I don't know what to say. But I envy you.

> *Leonidik stares at Marat for a moment and then walks out.*

Lika (*softly*) I've been worried about you.

Marat (*affectionately*) Truly?

Lika You've changed. You're not like you used to be. You're pulling away from me. Please don't. Remember how good it was for us?

Marat How could I forget? (*Pause.*) It's you that's pulling away, not me. Sometimes I think you're completely gone.

Lika No. (*lovingly*) I'm here, Marik. – What's the matter? Are you crying?

Marat (*fiercely*) I hate myself.

Lika (*astonished*) Why?

Marat Oh, to hell with it! (*pacing up and down*) Listen to me! You've got to give up the Komsomol. You're capable of more. I've had a word about you at the hospital. They'll take you as a trainee.

Lika When did they put that bandage on?

Marat At dawn.

Lika Then I'll change it.

Marat There's no need. At the hospital you'll witness things that will break your heart. But it's got to be done, do you understand?

Lika I'm still going to change that bandage. I've got my first-aid pack.

Marat I don't want you to! Get it? You'll be a trainee for a couple of months, you'll sit some exams, you'll progress. You'll be doing some good. Do we have unanimous agreement?

Lika Yes. But the wound must be cleaned, Marik . . .

She takes him by the arm.

Marat Don't! It's not necessary!

Lika I know how. The comrades at the Centre taught me. I'll do it beautifully.

Marat (*beaten*) Oh, bloody hell, all right.

Leonidik returns and stands in the doorway, watching. Lika sits Marat down and starts to undo the bandage.

Lika Now don't move. – Was he strong, the Nazi?

Marat Yup.

Lika Very big?

Marat Normal size.

Lika removes the bandage and looks at the arm for a long time.

Well, normal for a Nazi, which is – oh, hello!

Marat sees Leonidik. Lika turns and sees him too.

Lika That's a rotten deep wound. I'm going to clean it up. Sit still now . . . (*Her eyes meet Marat's.*) Does it hurt?

Marat A lot.

Lika (*cleans and re-bandages it*) It will get better.

Leonidik goes to Marat and hits him lightly on the shoulder.

Leonidik Put a brave face on it, old chap.

Lika (*fiercely*) Don't you touch him.

SCENE SIX

4 May. A bright sunny day. Lika is alone. She's been doing her laundry. Marat enters. An uncomfortable pause.

Marat Good morning!

Lika We've said good morning already.

Marat So we have. (*Pause.*) Where's Leonidik?

Lika He went for a walk. The doctor said he can start work tomorrow.

Marat Good for the doctor! Good for Leonidik! And good for us. He owes it to us.

Lika gives a weary sigh.

Shall I belt up?

Lika Whatever you like.

Marat Have you been to the hospital?

Lika I've no need of your advice, thank you. – Why are you back so early?

Marat We stopped the war for a tea break.

Lika Don't you ever give up?

Marat (*shyly*) Look at me.

Lika (*continuing with the laundry*) Why?

Marat You haven't looked at me for six days.

Lika Saved any more girls from drowning? Or caught another parachutist?

Marat Four of each! (*He clenches his fists and drops his head.*)

Lika How can you clown around like this? There's so much suffering, children starving to death next door, corpses piled up at the graveyards, and you . . . (*fiercely*) Tell me the truth. What's the scratch on your arm?

Marat . . . I slipped and fell on a roll of barbed wire.

Lika (*relaxing*) I guessed it was something like that. . . . It's good they put iodine on the cut; it won't get infected. (*with exaggerated concern*) Poor little boy . . .

Marat Lika . . .

Lika Shut up! I was ashamed. And I told Leonidik a lie: 'What a deep wound . . . ' Makes me sick to think of it! And you didn't say anything. Still hoping I'd believe you . . . (*plaintively*) How could you have done it, if you had the slightest feeling for me? – Why are you laughing?

Marat Who said I was laughing?

Lika Bugger off! You've no idea how much I despise you!

Marat Despise me?

Lika Yes! It's over now. All over!

Marat (*to himself*) Dead right.

Lika (*spinning*) What did you say?

33

Marat I said it's over!

Lika takes her laundry basket and goes out. Marat gets his suitcase and quickly packs a few things. He takes a piece of paper, and, placing it on top of the suitcase, writes fast. Leonidik enters and sees him.

Leonidik What are you doing here at this time of day?

Pause. Marat keeps writing.

Two more tram-lines are running. And the water's on in the house next door. Have we you to thank for that?

Marat Right, come over in the sunlight, let's have a look at you. Oh, Leonidik, you lovely blue-eyed boy . . .

He unexpectedly hugs Leonidik, then goes to the bed and places his note on Lika's pillow.

See that she gets that, will you?

Marat takes his suitcase and runs for the door.

Leonidik Where are you going, Marat?

Marat (*cheerily*) To the baths!

Marat exits fast. Pause. Lika enters.

Lika Where was he racing off to?

Leonidik He's quite mad . . . Said he was going to the baths . . . A lie, of course.

Lika is silent for a moment. Then she weeps bitterly.

What is it, Lika? Lika? You mustn't . . . my darling, you mustn't . . .

Lika (*taking his hand*) Listen, Leonidik. I may . . . love him.

Leonidik . . . I don't think there was any need to tell me that.

Lika He's always lying! . . . He made up the story about the parachutist. Only a scratch on his arm. I covered up for him. I was ashamed! I can't cover up any more. – Talk to him! You're our closest friend.

Leonidik You're such a pair of idiots! (*hesitantly*) I mean, in the midst of this tragedy, to . . . (*cross with himself*) Fair enough. None of it matters. You're still children.

Lika Children! We're not children.

Leonidik . . . He left you a note.

He gives her the note. She wipes her tears.

Lika What fibs has he made up now? (*Reads.*) 'To you and to Leonidik.' It's to both of us. (*Gives him the note.*) You read it.

Leonidik (*reads*) 'All right, it's true, I didn't catch a parachutist. But I did meet Major Artemov, and we had a long chat that night. Waiting for the call-up in the autumn's a fat lot of use, isn't it? He agrees with me, and so this is goodbye. Vengeance is mine! I promise you'll hear of me. Good luck to you, Lika, and Leonidik, don't lose heart. Be at the hospital tomorrow, Lika! Over and out.'

Lika Marik . . . (*Takes the note and stares at it.*) No, he's lying . . . He's always lying! I don't believe him. He'll be back.

Leonidik Not this time.

Lika How do you know?

Leonidik He's grown up. (*Shrugs.*) Happens to everyone.

Lika Do you want to go, too?

Leonidik Well, he went. So that's the only thing I can do now. He hasn't left me any alternative.

Very distant gunfire.

Lika Oh God! (*She clutches at him.*)

Leonidik Why are you frightened? That was a long way off.

Lika Every shot will be aimed at him now. Just at him.

Leonidik . . . He's lucky.

End of Act One.

Interval.

Act Two

SCENE SEVEN

*27 March 1946. Still the same room, but unrecognisable.
The war is over and life is back to normal. Evening.
Lika, now nearly twenty, an independent young woman,
sits comfortably on the sofa with textbooks and lecture
notes spread out around her. The wireless is on, giving
the weather forecast for the whole of the Soviet Union.
It takes a while. The telephone rings. Lika turns off the
wireless and lifts the receiver.*

Lika Hello? Yes? Hello? (*Pause.*) That's an impressive
silence. Any chance of breaking it, whoever you are?
(*stunned*) What! You? When? Yes, yes, got the telegram
yesterday! Course I'm not afraid! I haven't seen you for
years, and you ring from the phone in the hall . . .?
Come up at once, idiot! – By the way, the lift's working.

*She replaces the phone, jumps up and paces excitedly.
She laughs; then she grows sad. She looks at herself in
the mirror. She makes a start on tidying the room, but
then she hears the bell in the hall. She goes out and
comes straight back.*

Well, come in.

*Leonidik enters, wearing the greatcoat of a Red Army
private. He has matured, and is very altered.*

Leonidik Wait.

*He walks to the armchair, sits, puts his hand over his
eyes.*

Lika Say something, then.

Leonidik uncovers his eyes, smiles, and stands up to face her.

Leonidik May I kiss you?

Lika kisses him impetuously.

I've dreamed about this moment for four years.

They hold hands. He looks around.

It's all so different. My camp bed was here, the stove was here . . .

Lika Won't you take your coat off?

Leonidik Thing is . . . he can't manage terribly well.

He takes the coat off with some difficulty, and Lika sees that he has an artificial left arm.

So. There we are.

Lika (*smiles*) Fair enough. The war. It's as it should be.

Leonidik Yes, fair enough. (*Smiles.*) That's why I mumbled rubbish on the phone. I didn't want to scare you.

Lika My goodness, I've seen worse. I'd say you were pretty lucky.

Leonidik Not that lucky. I lost it a week before they surrendered. Bit of a pity, that. I did write to you that I was wounded. I wrote from Manchuria. I wrote from Khabarovsk. (*embarrassed*) But we won't go into details.

Lika All right.

Leonidik (*laughs*) Heavens, am I really back? Have I come back just like that?

Lika (*laughing*) You have! I promise you!

Leonidik When he saw Nevsky Prospect this morning . . . When he saw the sky over Leningrad . . . there's nowhere like it in the world, you know! – Do I sound mad?

Lika No, not at all. . . . I understand.

Leonidik (*gives her a parcel*) For you.

Lika (*opens it*) Slippers?

Leonidik From Japan. And look. This comb. Isn't it something?

Lika pins the comb into her hair in front of the mirror.

Lika (*laughing*) Straight out of *Madame Butterfly*! It's gorgeous! Oh, you – you're attentive, you're wonderful, you're terrific. (*She kisses him on the cheek.*) Want some tea?

Leonidik Love some.

Lika plugs in an electric kettle.

Lika We'll have to wait.

They sit and look at each other in silence.

What shall we talk about?

Leonidik How you have lived. All that has happened.

Lika I sometimes think there is nothing that hasn't happened. Everything that could possibly happen has happened. (*Pause.*) You know it all from my letters. You both joined up, my mother got killed, so . . . so I couldn't leave Leningrad, could I? Where would I go? So I worked at the hospital, and studied. The shelling was a nuisance. But that's how I lived. (*She smiles.*)

Leonidik And now?

39

Lika Second year of medical school.

Leonidik You've got everything you hoped for?

Lika . . . Not quite.

Leonidik Better keep trying, then. (*He takes her hand.*)

Lika (*laughs*) Not everything's under our control.

Leonidik That's undeniable. But everything will be fine.

Lika Think so?

Leonidik Sure of it.

He holds her hand a little longer than is appropriate.

Lika Kettle's boiling.

Leonidik Clever kettle!

Lika Why?

Leonidik Boiled in the nick of time.

Lika busies herself making the tea.

Lika Where are you staying?

Leonidik My cousin's. He was evacuated. Came back last spring. What's this jam?

Lika Quince.

Leonidik My cousin's weird. I don't expect we'll get on. (*cheerily*) Actually you're the only one left, the only one in the whole wide world.

Lika Just me?

Leonidik You and Marat. The three of us. That winter of '42. Nobody could forget it. Is that true?

Lika It is true.

They're silent, sunk in memories.

Leonidik Nice jam.

Lika More?

Leonidik Yes, please. Remember I ate that honey your mother sent you?

Lika (*smiles*) Marat was a bit miffed.

Leonidik No, he wasn't. He pretended to be. He gave me his food all the time. Funny old Marat . . . (*He stares at her.*)

Lika Yes. (*Pause.*) What will you do?

Leonidik He isn't sure yet.

Lika He's got an inkling, presumably?

Leonidik He has the possibility of working on a newspaper. He was a frontline journalist for three years. But that would only be a stopgap. Because he's brought home a suitcase full of poems.

Lika Any good ones?

Leonidik No, not yet. Some contenders are beginning to appear.

Lika I think we may call that progress. (*She smiles.*)

Leonidik I was with the shock troops for the first year. In the teeth of the war. Incredible, that I was spared. Incredible! Had friends, too; but I'm the only one left alive. I was always lucky, from the moment I walked into this room and ate your parcel.

Lika Aren't you still?

Leonidik I suppose so. Well, I've just eaten all your jam, so I must be. (*Indicates his false arm.*) My luck ran out just once.

Lika (*softly*) How did it happen?

Leonidik I caught a parachutist.

Lika You're joking!

Leonidik 'Fraid not.

Lika (*laughing*) If that's true, it's hilarious!

Leonidik He still hasn't written?

Lika No. I have only had three telegrams from him. On my birthday. In '43, in '44, in '45.

Leonidik Just greetings telegrams? Didn't give his address?

Lika No. (*a note of despair*) No! – Leonidik . . .! (*She takes his hand.*) Do you think he's alive?

Leonidik Presumably we'll find out in a fortnight's time. When your birthday comes around . . .

Lika He wouldn't forget us, would he?

Leonidik (*firmly*) He wouldn't dare.

Lika (*with a calm conviction*) He's been killed.

Leonidik No, he's just odd.

Lika Stay with me. For old time's sake, stay with me. I'll rig up a screen.

Leonidik (*laughs, and kisses her forehead*) Thanks, but I'll go to my cousin's.

Lika You aren't leaving?

Leonidik I've drunk the tea and eaten the jam. What would I want to stay for?

Lika (*seriously*) Are you an idiot?

Leonidik (*seriously*) Yes.

Lika Come tomorrow, then.

Leonidik Is that an order?

Lika Absolutely.

Leonidik Then I'll come. (*He tries to put on his greatcoat. It's a struggle.*)

Lika Let me help –

Leonidik No! He must learn to do things for himself! (*Smiles.*) Or he's totally screwed. (*With difficulty, he gets the coat on.*) Victory!

   They go to the door.

Lika It's very strange. We haven't actually told each other anything.

Leonidik You think not?

   Again they're silent, looking at each other.

I'll see you tomorrow. (*He goes quickly.*)

SCENE EIGHT

17 April. The end of the day, but the room is still full of spring sunshine. Leonidik is settled cosily on the window sill, reading a book. Lika enters.

Lika Hello!

Leonidik Hello! You're half an hour late!

Lika Committee meeting. – How did you get in?

Leonidik Over the last three weeks I've ingratiated myself with every single one of the neighbours. They'll even let me in at night, now.

Lika You're quite a man, aren't you?

Leonidik Oh, the public adore me. I've charmed all the old dears on your landing. One of them enquired when I was moving in.

43

Lika (*stops smiling*) What did you reply?

Leonidik . . . I referred her to Comrade Medical Probationer Vasilyevna for further information.

Lika . . . Not one of your best jokes.

Leonidik (*glum*) Sorry.

Lika Did you pick up the cinema tickets?

Leonidik (*nods*) Nine o'clock. But I'm not sure I want to go now.

Lika (*softly*) Look, don't be cross.

Leonidik I'm not cross. But it's pretty bloody awkward for me, isn't it?

Lika We're not going to talk about it.

Leonidik Fair enough, let's talk about something else. I have a plan. I thought dinner first, in a restaurant – not too expensive, perhaps, but not a greasy spoon. A glass or two. What do you think?

Lika Fine. – You know you're drinking really rather a lot.

Leonidik If you think I'm drinking to drown my sorrows, I'm clearly not drinking enough.

Lika Oh, God.

Leonidik Am I boring you?

Lika Starting to. And your health isn't great, you must accept that. I've booked you into the clinic for a check-up.

Leonidik Am I on my last legs?

Lika Listen, the war's over, Leonidik. It's time to be sensible.

Leonidik Fair enough. But tonight we'll get stewed.

Lika Why?

Leonidik Celebrating. (*Takes some money from his pocket.*) He has received an advance.

Lika (*delighted*) You sold some poems?

Leonidik He has sold a satirical piece about the sanitation in his apartment block.

Lika (*disappointed*) I thought perhaps . . . your proper work . . .

Leonidik You don't get paid for poetry. But anyway, let's get drunk. We'll have some of that Moldavian wine, the one called 'Lidya', after you. You drank a whole bottle on your birthday.

Lika Yes. And I cried in the restaurant. What a performance!

Leonidik (*cautiously*) Maybe the telegram will come . . .

Lika No, it's three days. It's not wartime, the post is working perfectly. Three days! There won't be a telegram. I just want to know why! Has he forgotten us? Or is he dead? (*tetchily*) What's your opinion, comrade?

Leonidik Don't be cross with me. I can't help it that I've come back alive . . . and he hasn't.

Lika Don't you think he'll come back?

Leonidik doesn't answer.

Fine. Why should you? You don't want Marat around, do you?

Leonidik (*angrily*) What are you saying?

Lika You know what I'm saying!

45

Leonidik That's enough, Lika!

Lika (*sinking into a chair*) Oh, it's so awful . . .

Leonidik takes his coat down from the rack.

Leonidik I'd better be going.

Lika No! Don't. I'll feel rotten if you leave now.

Leonidik Then I'll stay.

Lika Thank you. You're wonderful.

Leonidik Wonderful, attentive, and terrific?

Lika . . . You think I still love him, don't you? Actually I've nearly forgotten him. But it's as though I belong to the little girl I was in 1942, that brave, happy little girl . . . I have to obey her will . . .

Leonidik Let's get out in the sunshine.

Lika Please don't think I'm not happy now. I'm studying for the best profession in the world, I'm going to be a doctor! What can go wrong? (*cheerfully*) Come on, let's go.

She takes his coat and decides to help him on with it.

Leonidik Don't! I told you, don't help him! He has to do it by himself!

Lika Sorry.

There's a ring at the door. They both look round. Lika goes into the hall, as Leonidik struggles into his coat. She comes back.

A boy brought me a note. (*Reads it.*) Marat!

Leonidik What? Where is he?

Lika gives him the note.

(*Reads.*) 'I'm downstairs. If you want, I'll come up. Or tell the boy if you don't want to see me. And I'll vanish. Hero of the Soviet Union Marat Yevstigneyev.'

Lika (*whispers*) He's alive.

Leonidik See?

Lika (*galvanised*) Where's the boy? I must tell him!

Lika runs out.

Leonidik (*smiles*) Marik.

He takes out a comb and combs his hair. Lika comes back.

Lika The light bulb's gone.

Leonidik Stop worrying.

Lika . . . I've opened the front door. Is that all right, do you think, dear Leonidik?

Leonidik What's got into you?

Lika My head's spinning. (*She paces the room.*) I'll go and meet him.

Lika makes for the door just as Marat enters. He wears the dress uniform of a Guards captain. Strangely, he has hardly changed. He's still a boy, though his skin is weatherbeaten. He sees Lika, and they stand in silence for a few moments.

Marat Hello there!

Lika You're alive?

Marat Absolutely! (*He moves towards her, but then he notices Leonidik.*) You?

Marat goes to Leonidik and hugs him. They kiss on both cheeks.

47

We've been damn lucky, haven't we, my friend?

Leonidik Could've been a lot worse.

Marat What did you do?

Leonidik Infantry. Then war correspondent. You?

Marat Intelligence.

Lika Marat! Have you forgotten me?

Marat No, but he's a soldier, isn't he? (*He kisses Lika.*) Well, there we are. Just let them try and beat us now!

Lika Who?

Marat I don't know. Our enemies.

> *Marat has thrown off his greatcoat. Leonidik admires his decorations.*

Leonidik Look at that, he's got a star!

Marat (*to Lika*) So what did you think had happened?

Lika Why didn't you write?

Marat Many reasons. But the crucial thing is, I came back. Nothing else matters. (*to Leonidik*) Isn't that right? – Now hold on for one minute. (*He is looking at the two of them together.*) You haven't gone and got married, have you?

Leonidik The Matrimonial Affairs Sub-Committee has yet to reach agreement on this contentious issue.

Marat That's terrific, chaps!

Lika I waited and waited . . . three days ago . . . for a telegram.

Marat Yes, but that would've completely spoilt my entrance, wouldn't it?

Lika I think he stole that star, Leonidik.

Marat (*outraged*) I beg your pardon?

Lika And I thought he'd been killed . . .

Marat You don't know me. (*to Leonidik*) She doesn't, does she?

> *Marat slaps Leonidik on the arm and falls silent, realising the arm is artificial.*

Gosh, I'm sorry.

Leonidik (*shrugs*) Nothing to be done.

Marat Can't say I like it.

Leonidik (*smiles*) Can't say I do either.

Marat (*sharply*) Well I like it even less than you do.

Leonidik Why?

Marat . . . Another time.

Leonidik (*to Lika*) I have a few things to get from the market. I'll shoot off. Might have a quick drink whilst I'm at it . . .

Marat You didn't think I'd come empty-handed, did you?

> *Marat produces a bottle of cognac from his greatcoat.*

Leonidik Well, look at that.

Marat (*laughing*) What did you take me for?

> *Lika fetches glasses as Marat opens the bottle.*

Lika, you're not just beautiful, you're too beautiful, it's hurting my eyes. It's like staring at the sun. (*Marat pours three shots of cognac.*)

Leonidik (*raising his glass*) What shall we drink to?

They all think.

Marat Let's drink in silence.

They all knock back their shots. Marat immediately pours three more shots, and they all raise their glasses and knock them back. Marat begins to pour again.

SCENE NINE

2 May. Another sunny day. The windows are wide open. Distant music from loudspeakers down in the street. Marat paces restlessly. Lika sits and listens.

Marat I flew in on a Douglas from Berlin. Visibility was perfect, yet all I could see was destruction. Right across Russia, total carnage. Desolation. (*with quiet fury*) In the autumn I'll enrol at the Technical Institute. Hell, I will! And then we can start building bridges. That's my holy crusade: bridges. Things that join. (*Pause.*) I'll be twenty-two any minute. I used to think that was old. Not now, though. God, remember the dreams we had, back in '42!

Lika We were raw. We bared ourselves. Like film exposed to the light.

Marat Two weeks back, when I walked in here, I didn't realise how complicated it all is. We took Berlin a year ago, but it's only now, in Leningrad, that I believe the war is over.

Lika Does that make you sad?

Marat Scared, more like.

Lika Scared?

Marat Well, I suppose I mean lonely . . . As if I'd lost my family all over again. (*Pause.*) No one left.

Lika No one?

Marat I'm sorry. Suppose I'll just have to get used to it.

Lika Get used to what?

Marat Life. You. (*Laughs.*) Sometimes I'm not convinced that I am really alive. And that you are really you.

Lika Come here. Convince yourself.

Marat (*introverted*) Four years . . . seems like four decades sometimes . . . things one can't forget . . .

Lika Have you been . . . in love with anyone?

Marat This and that. Not worth discussing. – You know, it's funny. I've gone half way round the world and back again, and I still don't understand a damn thing about who I am. Do you understand anything? About who you are?

Lika Yes, everything!

Marat Everything? (*sternly*) You delude yourself, Lika. (*Pause.*) That's a lovely necklace you have.

Lika You gave it to me.

Marat That's not true. When did I do that?

Lika Last year, on my birthday. An old woman was selling it in Sadovaya Market. I admit I chose it and paid for it, but I knew it was from you.

Marat Well – thanks. (*Pause. He moves away.*) Did you just make that up?

Lika Maybe.

Marat Still . . . it's a very sweet thought.

> *Marat's at the window. The waltz to which they danced in '42 is heard on the loudspeakers in the street.*

Remember that?

Lika (*quietly*) Yes.

They stand and listen.

And then Leonidik walked in.

Marat And ate your parcel. Where is he, by the way? We said three o'clock.

Lika He'll be here. He's punctual.

Marat He's changed. I was the eldest in '42. Not now.

Lika Not then either.

Marat Whatever you say . . . (*Pause.*) I think of him often.

Lika So do I.

Marat I want him to be all right.

Lika So do I. Very much.

Marat Are his poems any good?

Lika (*thinks*) They're a bit labyrinthine.

Marat Is that good or bad?

Lika Risky, maybe . . . During the war I liked Turgenev. Used to read like mad. Turgenev and Tolstoy. But now for some inexplicable reason I find I only want to read children's books. Silly books, you know, for kids . . .

Marat (*somewhere else*) I really would like him to be happy.

Lika He had bad luck with that arm.

Marat No, that was my bad luck. – Has he told you he loves you?

Lika No. Not in so many words.

Marat But it is obvious.

Lika You know, you haven't told me either.

Marat If you can wait, I might tell you.

Lika Only might?

Marat Well, I'm not doing it in public . . . Would it be worth my while?

Lika Tell me first, and then we'll see.

Marat Leonidik holds higher trumps than me.

Lika I'm sorry?

Marat Lika, I'm horribly proud. I'm so proud I disgust myself. They've given me a vile little room at the hostel. Do I complain? No, I'm a hero, aren't I! Heroes don't complain!

Lika Marik, I've been meaning to say this for ages – this is your room, by rights, and if you –

Marat Oh, for God's sake belt up. I don't want to hear about that.

Lika (*laughing at him*) So, one day they had a rip-roaring argument about the housing allocation.

Marat They didn't have an argument. That's half the trouble.

Leonidik comes in at a run.

Leonidik Konitiva! Konitiva! That's 'good day' in Japanese. (*He bows ceremoniously*.) And now the distribution of the presents for the first of May. Snowdrops for the young lady, and a yo-yo for the Red Army hero. (*He gives them presents*.) What larks for the children of the revolution! (*to Marat*) Later on, we'll raffle the special prize.

Marat You're sloshed, Mr War Correspondent.

Leonidik Only had the one bottle, and that was with my creepy cousin. (*Slams on the table another bottle he has brought.*) More is required to finish the job.

Lika I'm going to kick you out.

Leonidik Marat won't let you. Marat loves me. He's a friend of the people, is Marat. (*He blows a shrill blast on a toy whistle.*) Marat, tell her you love me. And then give me the bloody corkscrew.

Marat Give him the corkscrew.

Lika Not likely! I've had him examined by specialists. He has a dozen separate complaints, and his heart isn't worth ten kopeks.

Leonidik He's going to die soon –

Lika Cretin.

Leonidik – so give him the corkscrew.

Lika No.

Leonidik First of May – Workers' International Holiday!

Lika No.

Leonidik Meeting of two comrades-in-arms!

Lika This has been going on for a fortnight.

Leonidik (*pleading*) It's the last time! I'll never get drunk again!

Lika (*handing him the corkscrew*) It'd better be the last time.

Leonidik You can count on me, sweetheart. (*He goes to the window, opening the bottle.*) It's like before the war out there. Flags on the battleships, music, dancing – as if these five years hadn't happened, as if all the chaos had never been!

54

Marat But it has. (*to Lika*) Remember that argument we had? I wanted everything to be the same after the war. But you were right, as I realised this morning, watching the parade. The bands were playing just like before, the troops were marching, the tanks and half-tracks rattling by, parents holding up children to watch. But what it meant . . . what it meant was different. Suddenly I understood: we've entered a new age. Meaning, the past is not coming back.

Lika Maybe we've changed . . .

Leonidik 'We'? Who's 'we'? Be intriguing to find out, wouldn't it, who 'we' are?

Lika 'We' are the grown-ups who read children's books.

Leonidik I was in the East when they dropped the atom bomb on Hiroshima. That day something became clear to me: 'we' are the survivors.

Marat (*fiercely*) No! The victors! We are the victors! If we ever forget that, they will trample us into the earth.

Leonidik Intoxicating stuff, victory, isn't it, old chap? Watch out when you sober up. Let me tell you the single greatest danger of being victorious.

Marat Go ahead.

Leonidik That we take on the vices of the defeated.

Marat You never used to do so much thinking, Leon. Sure it's good for you?

Leonidik Take note, Lika – Marat doesn't want me to think. He's a dictator. He's taking over Russia, like a Cossack, at the gallop – tally ho!

Lika Stop arguing! It's dreary.

Leonidik Oh, you're siding with the dictator? Perfect. I love you for the clarity of your thought, Lika. Did you hear? I just said I love you. (*Shouts*.) Did everybody hear? I made an announcement!

Marat It does look as though he shouldn't have any more alcohol.

Leonidik Oppression! I'm being oppressed! – And so, comrades, we've debated the nature of victory in war. Next item: what is love, and how do you cook it?

Lika Don't, don't . . .

Leonidik Attention, attention! The speaker is Marat – the Hero of the Soviet Union, the subject: love! Over to you, sir.

Marat (*goes up to him*) You talk an awful lot of shit. If you must know – a real man can do without love.

Leonidik Brilliant! – How do you become a real man?

Lika Marat gives lessons.

Leonidik Put me down from three till five on Sundays. It wouldn't hurt me to try.

Marat You're beyond help.

Leonidik (*squaring up to him*) Now don't start taking liberties . . .

Lika (*worried*) Boys, please stop this . . .

Leonidik Ah, yes. All the girls love a Hero of the Soviet Union.

Marat Yup. And they can't stand a piss-artist.

Without warning, Leonidik swings a punch with his good arm. He connects with Marat's jaw. Marat goes down heavily.

Leonidik Only lost the one arm, you know.

Lika (*rushing to Marat*) What have you done? Brute!

Leonidik sits at the table and ties on his napkin.

Leonidik I'm starving. What's for lunch?

Marat struggles to sit up. Lika helps him.

Lika A fine pair you are! Coming to blows!

Leonidik He got what he was asking for, that's all.

Marat Damn it, that hurt.

Lika Here, drink some water.

Marat Forgive me, Leon. I went too far.

Leonidik It's nothing. I wasn't expecting such luck.

Marat (*rubbing his chin*) Yes . . . blindingly good.

Lika Idiots! What do you mean?

Marat I mean I underrated my opponent.

Leonidik (*eating*) Yes, and he'll thrash you next time, too.

Marat See, Lika? He's threatening me again!

Lika What's that to a real man who can do without love?

SCENE TEN

26 May. Late evening, but it's still light outside. A wonderful patch of golden sky is visible through the open window. Marat and Leonidik are waiting for Lika.

Leonidik What's the time?

Marat Quarter past ten. She must be having fun. (*Pause.*) Shall I turn on the light?

Leonidik Why? Tonight there will be no darkness.

Marat Are you being poetic?

Leonidik Don't be cruel. The white nights are miraculous.

Marat Think we should go home? It's late.

Leonidik You go home if you want. (*Indicates himself.*) He's staying. He hasn't seen her for two days. He's missed her, and he's not afraid of admitting it. Know why? Because he isn't a real man. His emotions are out in the open.

Marat What's it like out there? Chilly?

Leonidik It's fine. (*Pause.*) You were just going, weren't you?

Marat (*looks out of the window*) You're right, it is a miracle. That sky . . . all green and gold. . . . Leonidik, have you ever been to Saratov?

Leonidik Passed through.

Marat Like it?

Leonidik So-so.

Marat I may be going there. To study.

Leonidik You're out of your mind. Why?

Marat A friend has invited me. A comrade from the war. (*Smiles.*) They say the Volga's very broad there.

Leonidik So what?

Marat So it's a beautiful place. And I'm getting fed up with your company. (*very serious*) How do you feel about me?

Leonidik I can't imagine life without you, sweetheart.

Marat Don't joke. I love you.

Leonidik (*simply*) I know.

Marat But it doesn't alter anything, all right?

Leonidik All right.

Marat One of us has got to go.

Leonidik Fair enough.

Marat Leon . . . Why don't you go? It'd be better.

Leonidik Who would it be better for?

Marat You. Absolutely. You.

Leonidik (*laughs*) Will I become a real man if I go?

Marat Who knows? Look, we mustn't lie to each other, she doesn't love you and that's that.

Leonidik Quite possibly, but we're still going to ask her.

Marat That might not be very clever . . .

Leonidik But can't you see, Citizen Marat, that he who has nothing is still afraid? Afraid to lose the little nothing he's got?

Lika enters, turning on the light.

Lika Why are you sitting in the dark?

Leonidik It's nice. With the white night outside.

Lika I thought you would've both gone home. You're very persistent, aren't you?

Marat Leonidik's the persistent one.

Lika Yes, well, you were going to run away, weren't you? Fine – off you go. Leonidik and I are going to have tea. I've bought him some quince jam.

Leonidik Hear that?

Marat Women! Christ! (*cheerily*) Very well, I'll have tea as well.

Lika First say you're sorry you wanted to go.

Marat Shit.

> *His holster is hanging up. He goes to it and takes out his pistol.*

If you don't give me some tea, I'll shoot this Leonidik of yours. (*He aims.*)

Lika (*laughing*) Idiots! What idiots you are! (*She prepares the tea.*) This city is so magical. The lilac's out in the Field of Mars . . . the scent's fabulous. And the sun sinking over the Fortress was the colour of a just-ripe peach. Down by the river, young lovers are sitting on stone benches, holding hands. When there's no night the place goes mad . . .! Just now I saw a couple kissing on the next landing. (*to Marat*) Guess who? Lelya from Tbilisi.

Marat I'll throttle her, shall I? – Do you write love poems, Leon?

Leonidik Sometimes.

Marat (*to Lika*) Any good?

Lika Not bad.

Marat Everyone loves a love poem, don't they?

Leonidik Unfortunately, they're not for publication.

Marat Who are they for, then?

Leonidik Me.

Marat Ah, so you're able to tell before you write them – this for public consumption, this for my private pleasure?

What's that, the artistic equivalent of double-entry book-keeping?

Leonidik A true poet must experiment. Take a few risks. Pointless to involve the readers, who simply aren't prepared.

Marat Not every reader's a coward, you know. Maybe they'd like to take a few risks with the poet? Maybe this voyage into the unknown of his would be best not undertaken alone!

Lika Will you stop shouting. Sit down and wait till the kettle boils. Marat, you attack Leonidik about nothing at all. Why do we like what we do? Because it makes us try things, make mistakes, work it out. The most risky profession of all is medicine. Which is why I love it. When my mother was young, she dreamt of becoming a great scientist. She didn't make it . . . But me . . . You see, children are born to succeed where their parents have failed. That's what I think. So I promise you that there will be no diseases left on the planet at the end of the twentieth century. On that, I give you my word.

Marat I'd rather you gave me some salami. Talk about having a big head!

Lika As soon as I finish my degree I'll start a thesis. I sometimes wake up and think, who can stop me, now? Who can stop me becoming a great scientist? Who is the enemy?

Leonidik You, perhaps?

Lika I'm sorry?

Leonidik Perhaps the enemy is you yourself.

Lika No, hang on –

Leonidik They say you have to find the enemy in order to defeat him.

Marat We didn't have to find fascism. It came to us. What could be a worse enemy than that?

Leonidik Well, I don't know – a secret enemy's always more dangerous.

Marat You're both driving me insane. (*to Leonidik*) Since you stopped drinking you've been completely impossible. You believe all Lika's dire predictions. And she's only trying to scare you.

Lika That is not helpful. Leonidik is by nature nervy and physically weak. You should be backing me up, not goading him.

Marat (*grumpily*) But I can't have a drink, because of him, can I?

Lika . . . Despite all the jokes, I feel sad. Why is that, do you think?

Marat Shall I tell you?

Leonidik No, don't.

Marat (*to Leonidik*) You wanted it all to come out.

Leonidik She knows why we sometimes feel sad . . . When the three of us are together . . .

 Pause.

Lika Let's not pursue it.

Leonidik Sooner or later, we have to. He's thinking of going to Saratov.

Lika Are you?

Marat Yup. I will, too. You'll both have a weep when I'm gone. (*Pause.*) How peculiar: it has got dark after all.

Leonidik He told me I should go away. He said you didn't love me.

Lika . . . Marat knows everything about everything.

Guitar music is heard from outside.

Leonidik Who's that playing the guitar?

Lika My neighbour, on his balcony. He's very musical.

Marat Is he in love?

Lika Hopelessly. He's sixty, and he's getting married soon.

Leonidik Ah, a modern bridegroom. With all his arms and legs.

Marat Nicely put.

Lika (*to Marat*) You're going where?

Marat Saratov. Like it?

Lika Never been.

Leonidik Not a bad little town. Even got a medical school.

Marat Oh, it's got the lot.

Lika Is that why you chose it?

Marat I've a friend there.

Lika Haven't you any friends here?

Marat (*looking at Leonidik*) I have. That's half the trouble.

Leonidik (*smiles*) Nicely put.

Marat (*grimly*) Well, someone has to go.

Lika You have seniority.

Marat Ah yes. Intelligence officer.

Leonidik A real man.

Lika (*to Leonidik*) What about you?

Leonidik I'm not going anywhere. No! I'll only go if you make me!

Marat That's what he keeps saying, you see.

Lika (*sharply, to Marat*) Shut up!

Leonidik helps himself to some more jam.

Leonidik Quince . . . a curious phenomenon . . . I've never seen a quince actually growing.

Marat I have.

Leonidik (*to Lika*) I was lying. I'll stay with you even if you send me away.

Lika Oh yes, why is that?

Leonidik Because without you there is nothing.

Lika (*to Marat*) What do you say to that?

Marat (*grins*) No point grovelling, is there?

Leonidik Don't the neighbours mind you having two men in your room at this hour?

Lika We have nice neighbours. It's a good housing allocation.

Marat (*laughs*) What a daft expression. It's a room. Once I was horribly in love with a woman in Drogovich. As I was leaving she called after me, 'Marik, don't be silly, come back! I have such a marvellous housing allocation!'

Leonidik (*laughing*) Bravo!

Lika Leonidik, where have you been horribly in love?

Leonidik In Leningrad.

Lika (*to Marat*) You can't keep up with him, can you?

Marat No, I've no chance. Especially since you still adore Turgenev.

Lika I can't see how laughing at me helps.

Marat I'm not laughing, I'm crying. (*He gets up*.) Right, that's enough of all that. Someone's got to go. Me or him.

Leonidik (*to Lika*) You decide.

Lika Oh, I see. (*angrily*) Perhaps I'll choose the old man with the guitar . . .

Leonidik (*listening to the guitar*) Well, he's putting some effort into it.

Marat I've had enough of the stupid gags.

Lika Then let's be quiet for a moment. (*Pause.*) Marat, do you love me?

Marat is silent.

Leonidik He loves you. He told me.

Lika Oh, you're going to behave like a real man now, are you?

Leonidik It's catching . . .

Lika Don't tell me about him. Tell me about you.

Leonidik . . . If I lose you I shall be completely lost. You're everything to me. You're my whole universe.

Marat What's the use?

Lika goes to Leonidik and runs her hand through his hair.

Lika Want some more tea?

Leonidik (*weak smile*) Brandy would be better.

Marat (*pale*) I'll bring you both brandy tomorrow.

Lika stares out of the window.

Lika It's dawn already . . . What a short night . . .

End of Act Two.

Act Three

*10 December 1959. The same room, thirteen years later.
The furniture has changed, but it's not very expensive.
Snow is falling outside the window. The clock strikes
eleven. Lika and Leonidik come in from the street. Lika
helps Leonidik to take off his fur-lined overcoat, then
kneels and pulls off his boots, then goes behind a screen
and changes into her dressing-gown. Meanwhile Leonidik
changes his jacket and puts on his slippers. Lika plugs in
the kettle. Leonidik takes cheese from the sideboard. He
nibbles at it. Lika sees this and slaps his hand. Leonidik
sits at his desk and opens the newspaper. Lika starts
laying the table for supper.*

Leonidik (*reads*) 'LenElectric have enlarged their stocks
of metal crockery. Have you thought of replacing your
utensils before the holidays? . . . The Gastronome is
pleased to anounce a massive January sale. . . . Why not
see in the New Year at an Intourist Restaurant?'

Lika Bread's gone stale.

Leonidik (*reads*) 'Wireless programmes for the eleventh
of December: 4.45 – Comrades, open your hearts! Song
recital. 5.30 – Calling all Komsomols. 6.20 – The early
stages of rheumatism. 7.15 – Respected poet A. Sofronov
reads from his work.'

Lika (*kissing the top of his head*) That'll do.

Leonidik Fair enough. But wait – eight o'clock: 'What
joy to live in our Soviet Land!'

Lika Come and have your supper.

Leonidik Fair enough. (*He goes to the table.*)

Lika Want a sandwich?

Leonidik Why not?

Lika Cheese?

Leonidik Salami. (*Pause.*) I thought the play was rubbish.

Lika Why? It was just the same as usual. Short, though. Only three and a half hours.

Leonidik The people's artist was mugging all over the place. I don't know why you like him.

Lika He wasn't at his best.

Leonidik He shouldn't be allowed on a stage. He's like a puppet. (*Sips his tea.*) If I had my way, I'd close all the theatres.

Lika Why?

Leonidik Well, I suppose there isn't actually much wrong with the idea that everything that's good is good, and everything that's bad is bad . . . But let's just say it begins to pall with repetition.

Lika You're a free-thinker, that's your trouble.

She takes a box of chocolates from the sideboard.

Leonidik Well, look at that! What's it in honour of?

Lika My pay rise. Two hundred roubles a month from the first of January. Or have you forgotten?

Leonidik You might have provided something stronger for the occasion.

Lika You can put that thought straight out of your mind.

Leonidik Still, you keep your nose clean, you get promoted. That's good.

Lika You're not doing badly yourself, lately.

Leonidik I strive to serve the labouring masses.

Lika (*smiles*) Idiot.

Leonidik It's a decent trade, which forbids the intake of alcohol. Not chocolate, though. (*He eats one.*) So what is it you're going to be?

Lika Attached Supervisor.

Leonidik Marvellous! I knew what I was doing when I married you. What are you attached to?

Lika General practice. I teach and I practise.

Leonidik Which is better – to be attached, or unattached?

Lika Unattached, probably.

Leonidik So we still have goals to strive for! Hurray! – By the way, I had a word with the housing allocation manager. He's promised us a new apartment soon. With luck, we'll move in the spring. – Doesn't that please you?

Lika Yes, it does. (*quietly*) Except that I'm used to this room.

Leonidik Dear oh dear oh dear. Still, we're moving, all the same. Look at this useless old clobber! It looks like it's been here for ever! – But fair enough, who cares?

Lika Want some more tea?

Leonidik (*rising from the table and kissing her hand*) No, I'm finished, many many thanks. I'm going to work. Have to hand the proofs in tomorrow. By the way, I'm out of ink.

Lika I'll buy some, darling.

Leonidik And I'm out of carbon paper.

Lika I'll buy that too.

She clears the table. Leonidik sits at his desk and looks through his proofs.

Leonidik That bastard Petrov. An edition of five thousand copies? He promised me ten thousand. (*Smiles.*) Still, we don't have a book out every year. (*sharply*) I see your favourite layabout's getting an edition of a hundred thousand.

Lika He's not my favourite.

Leonidik You're always reading him.

Lika You liked him too. You used to.

Leonidik Well, he started very promisingly. Had something to say. And then? (*fiercely*) Cheap success! These ridiculously vast editions, year after year! It's completely changed his personality. (*He fumes.*)

Lika Don't do it to yourself, my dear. . . . If you like, I'll go and talk to Petrov. Sometimes it makes a difference. Five thousand is patently not enough.

Leonidik Why not? You deal with Petrov. You're my guardian angel. The most perfect wife in the world . . .

Lika Stop it. (*She strokes his hair.*) Now go to your desk.

Leonidik Sweet dreams, my lovely Attached Supervisor.

Lika (*kissing him*) Goodnight.

Lika turns off the light. There's just the lamp on the desk.

Do you mind if I play the tape machine?

Leonidik Not at all. Music helps me work.

*Lika switches on a reel-to-reel machine. We hear the
slow waltz to which she and Marat once danced.*

(*Smiles.*) Your favourite tune again?

Lika (*softly*) Don't you like it?

Leonidik It's not a bad little number.

SCENE TWELVE

*11 December, 3 p.m. – but December days are short in
Leningrad, and it's growing dark outside.*

*Home from her shift, Lika is busy with the housework.
She clears the table and goes behind the screen with a
loaded tray.*

*There's a light knock at the door. It's repeated. The
door opens slowly: it's Marat. He looks around, then
goes to the window and presses his forehead against
the glass.*

*Lika comes out from behind the screen and sees
Marat. They stare at each other for a long time.*

Lika (*softly*) What have you . . . What have you . . .
have you gone mad?

Marat No.

Lika It's futile.

Marat No it isn't.

Lika . . . So many years! You must understand!

Marat So many years what?

Lika So many years after.

Marat Well, what of it? (*Shouts.*) Stand still! Don't
move! Just stand there . . .

Lika Marat, take your hat off. (*He does so.*) You are . . .

Marat What am I?

Lika You're just like you. (*Pause.*) Have I got old, too?

Marat No. You'll always be beautiful. (*softly*) Once upon a time an old, old man lived with his old, old wife, in a little house in –

Lika Be quiet. (*Whispers.*) Can't you see my tears?

Marat I didn't know it was going to be like this.

Lika If you could feel the horror of it . . . No! Don't come any closer.

Marat I shan't.

Lika Stay by the window.

Marat All right.

Pause.

Lika Where do you live?

Marat Far away.

Lika As it should be. (*Smiles.*) Building bridges?

Marat Yes. (*Pause.*) When I come to Leningrad, I come here.

Lika Why?

Marat To look through my window. And then to go away.

Lika That's as it should be. Nothing's going to happen.

Marat I know.

Lika When's your train? Hurry up and go!

Marat I can't.

Lika Why not?

Marat I'm in a bad way. And since I'm here . . . (*rudely*) I mean, I didn't just come to see you, I came to see you both. (*softly*) You're all I have.

Lika But you're not going to start –

Marat No, no. You've been married thirteen years. I've been married quite a time myself.

Lika You're married?

Marat Why shouldn't I be?

Lika So therefore . . .

Marat Yes. Just as we decided.

Lika Leonidik blames you for going away. You haven't written once in thirteen years. He says you've forgotten us.

Marat Did you think I had?

Lika No. Might've been better if I did. (*affectionately*) What made you get married?

Marat I didn't. (*Laughs.*) See? I've got out of the habit of lying.

Lika . . . You said you're in a bad way?

Marat I'll tell you later. When Leonidik comes.

Lika Tell me now.

Marat No.

Lika Tell me!

   Pause.

Marat So, how are things?

Lika Fine.

Marat Work?

Lika Like I said – fine. Good clinic. Good area.

Marat General practice?

Lika (*apologetically*) Yes.

Marat But surely you wanted to –

Lika It didn't come off. But everything's fine. I've been promoted. Attached Supervisor of the unit.

Marat Attached?

Lika Leonidik thinks it's funny too.

Marat How is he?

Lika It's all going brilliantly. His third book of poems is about to come out. He isn't attacked by the press, or at rallies. And we're getting a new apartment. Moving in the spring.

Marat What about this room?

Lika I don't know. We'll let it.

Marat You could do that? After all we –? (*She's silent.*) So Leonidik has everything under control.

Lika He takes seminars at the university. He's in demand.

Marat (*cautiously*) Poets seem to be in the news a lot these days. Even the kids buy poetry. But I've never heard any arguments about him.

Lika He doesn't try to be fashionable.

Marat I bought that last slim volume of his. I see it was only a limited edition. But there are piles of them in the shops. (*Pause.*) Other writers have a print run of a hundred thousand, and you still can't lay hands on a copy.

Lika Cheap success. Not worth much.

Marat And his books, lying on the shelves, collecting dust – what kind of success is that?

Lika (*flares up*) Have you actually read his poems?

Marat (*nods*) He didn't make any mistakes. He didn't break any of the rules.

Lika He doesn't publish his best work.

Marat I see.

Lika What?

Marat (*harshly*) Everything.

Lika Marik, don't tell him you've read him . . . don't say anything.

Marat But that would be a lie.

Lika Then let it!

Marat (*sits down*) How do you live here? . . . I don't understand.

　　Leonidik opens the door and enters.

Leonidik Marat!

SCENE THIRTEEN

The same evening. They sat down to supper an hour ago, but they're still at it.

Leonidik It's not worth arguing about. You can never see yourself – who you are, what you are, whether you've achieved anything or whether you haven't . . . (*Pours himself some wine.*) Only death provides the answers. So here's to death!

Lika takes his glass from him, smiling.

Lika You mustn't drink any more.

Leonidik This woman persecutes me. She's been persecuting me for thirteen years! (*Laughs.*) That's what you get with a guardian angel. However, here we are, you appeared an hour ago, and it's as if you never went away. Why are you so quiet?

Marat . . . I spent my childhood in this room.

Leonidik And?

Marat (*smiles*) I don't know. (*Looks at them.*) Isn't it strange . . .?

Leonidik Isn't what strange?

Marat . . . There's a day that sticks in my memory. The first of May, 1934. The parade. I would have been nine. My dad marched beside me in a new uniform. He held tightly to my hand, and there was Kirov, standing on the rostrum, saluting, smiling . . . (*passionately*) If only everything could've stayed as it was!

Leonidik But after the thirties . . . came the forties . . .

Lika And the shame is, we saw more than we could understand, my poor Marik.

Marat Why do you call me poor?

Lika Because you believe in the impossible.

Marat Maybe the others who felt like me never came back from the war . . . (*He puts his head in his hands.*)

Leonidik (*gently*) Hey . . . what is it?

Marat (*studies the others carefully*) How do we live? I think about this all the time. I'm thirty-five, so are you . . . Lika's thirty-three . . . What have we done?

76

Lika . . . You've had a lot to drink.

Marat I've had just what's necessary! I'm no alcoholic, you don't have to stand guard over me!

Lika How many bridges have you built?

Marat Six.

Lika Is that too few or too many?

Marat It's enough.

Lika There, you see! And his poems get published! And I tend the sick! All that we dreamed about has happened. (*gaily*) Well? Aren't I right?

Marat I always believed what you said. But not this time.

Lika . . . What do you want from us?

Marat I wanted you to help me. (*a sour laugh*) Didn't realise you were worse off than I am.

Leonidik We lost everything in the siege. But we found each other. (*bitterly*) You'd no right to leave us!

Marat Weren't my reasons adequate?

Leonidik They might have been for an ordinary man. But you are the great Marat.

Marat I enjoy being flattered. But let's talk seriously.

Lika Oh, do let's. What's your apartment like? How many rooms?

Marat (*to Leonidik*) See? She's afraid.

Lika What am I afraid of?

Marat The truth.

Leonidik Very wearying in large doses, the truth.

77

Marat (*hotly*) Tell me this: when is a man finished? I'll tell you: when he suddenly realises that his whole life is fixed, he'll never be anything more than he is already. (*to Leonidik*) Are you tired of living?

Leonidik . . . I suppose I should tell the truth: I don't give a toss one way or the other.

Marat Don't try and be witty!

Leonidik . . . I am tired, yes.

Marat Why?

Leonidik Well, old chap, I'm sure you know it can be awfully tiring standing still.

Marat (*to Lika*) What have you done to him?

Lika (*angrily*) Dear friend, you have no right to use that tone of voice!

Marat Thirteen years ago I left you together in this room. The room where I spent my childhood. I'll use any tone of voice I like! Understand? – Are you happy?

Long pause.

Leonidik We get by.

Pause.

We visit the clinic regularly, our housing allocation is upgraded . . . (*He goes to Lika.*) The dreams of youth . . . who got in their way? Leonidik did. Not exactly a good result. – I write badly, don't I?

Marat You write correctly.

Leonidik You're very polite, comrade.

Lika (*alarmed*) Marat, what are you –

Marat Lika says you don't publish your best poems.

Leonidik I have been guilty of that.

Marat But you still write them?

Leonidik No, I've lost my touch. (*Laughs.*) He's such an arse. He published the dull little ditties, and kept the rest to himself, revising, pruning, tweaking a cadence here, a cadence there . . . But – to improve – a poet must get a reaction.

Marat How long have you know this?

Leonidik He's known it for ages; but he wouldn't admit it to himself.

Lika Shut up! Can't you see that Marat's determined to convince you your life is wasted? (*acidly*) Not very polite in front of a lady. Besides, for a judge, he's rather an interested party, isn't he?

Marat That was below the belt.

Leonidik . . . So Marat's a wicked breaker-up of marriages, but we're steaming along just fine, with everything coming up roses. I see.

Long pause.

Lika Marat, it's late. You should go.

Marat puts on his overcoat, and stands in the middle of the room, putting on his scarf and his cap.

Marat Perhaps it wasn't worth coming here, at all . . . (*He goes to the door, then turns back.*) I want to tell you about bridges! Bridges! The best type of engineering in the world! I've done six bridges! The six chapters of my life . . . But does any of them count as a real achievement? (*Pause.*) I had a friend. A design engineer. We built three bridges together. He was a confident chap, but he wasn't satisfied either. One day he was given a new bridge to design – a bridge without precedent, a fantastical structure!

79

Lot of people said it couldn't be done . . . But he managed to get me the post of works manager. It could have been my life's work! But it isn't. I abandoned my friend. Isn't that unthinkable? I left him to the wolves. I convinced myself I wasn't ready, couldn't do it, didn't have the experience . . . maybe that was true? But whether it was or it wasn't, I swiftly got myself transferred to another site. He wrote to me there: 'Hello, Marik, you extinct volcano . . .' That's what he called me. (*Pause. Swiftly*) Now he's in a very bad way. All the arse-lickers and yes-men are saying he had bad traits . . . over-ambitious, headstrong . . . the project should never have been started. – But the crucial point is that he despises me, maybe even hates me! I can't come to terms with that. I don't think I'll ever come to terms with that.

Leonidik That's a sad story. Pity it isn't believable.

Marat Why isn't it believable?

Leonidik Because it isn't logical.

Marat And life has to be logical, does it? Well, write a bloody poem about it, and get it printed in *Pravda*! Has all your life been logical?

Lika Darling Marik, we're not children any more. Our time is up in the land of dreams. We have to come down to earth.

Marat Don't want to!

Lika We aren't supermen.

Marat Who says we're not? – Oh, we're supposed to be grateful to be alive? Is that it? Well, think how many people died, so that we could live! Remember the blockade in the depth of winter, the suffering, thirty degrees below! The children's sledges piled high with bodies! Hundreds and hundreds of thousands perished, so that we could be happy, and extraordinary, and triumphant! And what are we? What are we now? – Try and remember what you were, Lika. Try and remember your promise. Where is it? Where is your promise? (*Pause.*) You've gone very quiet.

Lika . . . I'm afraid.

Marat (*strokes her hair affectionately*) At last. (*Smiles.*) Oh, Lika, Lika . . . sometimes it's good to be afraid. There are plenty of optimists who are scared out of their wits. (*Thinks hard.*) What I'm trying to tell myself is that on the brink of death it still isn't too late to start over.

Lika wants to object, but can't find the words. All she can do is smile, frightened and lost.

(*Cheerfully*) And now I shall try and be logical. Always a first time, Leonidik. I mean . . . I could tell you, Lika, I could tell you how I . . . damn it, I shall tell you! Listen: when I lost you I lost everything. (*He goes very close to her.*) The birds don't sing in the morning; the stars don't shine at night. The sky is empty. Understand? Not a single star! Just silence and darkness. Nothing. (*Pause.*) Well, there we are. You wanted your logic. You fools. (*to Lika*) How's it all going to turn out, I wonder?

Pause. Then Lika goes to Leonidik.

Lika (*firmly*) Just like before, only better. My husband will be happy. I promise you that.

Marat runs from the room.

Marat Goodbye! (*He's gone.*)

Leonidik Bring him back, Lika, bring him back!

Lika (*tears pouring down her face*) I can't . . . I can't . . .

SCENE FOURTEEN

31 December. The table is laid for a New Year's supper for two. Lika and Leonidik sit on the sofa, playing cards. Lika lays a final trump.

Lika How about that?

Leonidik (*lays down his cards*) He loses. What a fool.

Lika Third time in a row!

Leonidik Triple fool of the Soviet Union!

Lika You're just not attentive enough.

Leonidik Or wonderful enough, or terrific enough.

Lika But you have a gorgeous tie.

Leonidik Yes I do.

Lika What's the time?

Leonidik Nineteen sixty in a few minutes. (*Goes to the window.*) The citizens are hurrying home, to see in the New Year at table. Great crowds of them . . .

Lika It always brings childhood to mind . . .

Leonidik At midnight the streets will be empty. (*He is quiet.*)

Lika What are you thinking?

Leonidik Marat.

Lika Yes. He'll be alone. Five thousand miles away. (*Laughs.*) Three weeks gone, and that's that!

Leonidik He's a sweetheart.

Lika Don't.

Leonidik Right, let's have another game. Perhaps I'll get my revenge!

Lika (*smiling*) What's got into you today?

Leonidik They're coming, damn them, they're coming.

Lika Who?

Leonidik (*with a grimace*) The sixties.

Lika You are a fool. (*She kisses the top of his head.*)

Leonidik (*quietly*) Don't, my love.

Lika Why are you being so nice to me?

Leonidik I am, aren't I?

Lika You've been clowning around all evening . . . Won't you be bored? Greeting the New Year with just me for company?

Leonidik He won't be bored. (*Goes to the table.*) He's made a majestic salad. Why didn't he become a cook? 'Tis true, his life is wasted!

Lika Why do you keep looking at the clock?

The doorbell rings.

Leonidik That's it then. Open the door.

Lika looks at him with a puzzled expression.

That's it. All over.

A knock at the door.

Come in, Marik.

The door opens. Marat stands there, in his fur coat, covered in snow.

Lika . . . You?

Marat As you see.

Leonidik I was afraid you wouldn't . . . (*Slaps him on the back.*) But you never fail, do you? Marat, you're the friend of the people!

Marat How did you find my address?

Leonidik Brain-power. But I was afraid the aeroplane would be late. Now I can relax.

Lika What have you been up to? Tell me.

Leonidik Lika, I have something for you. Bit of a surprise. It's with the neighbours. But the hour has come, I'll fetch it.

Leonidik exits. Pause.

Lika . . . I thought I would never see you again.

Marat Me too. (*He takes her hand, hesitantly.*)

Lika Your hand is cold.

Marat It was tricky getting here from the airport. New Year's Eve. No taxis. (*He presses her hand to his cheek.*)

Lika . . . Are you sure you should have come?

Marat No, not really. But yesterday I got this telegram. (*He hands it to her.*)

Lika (*reads*) 'Catch first plane. Lika needs you. Arrive by thirty-first, no later. Leonidik.' – I didn't know about it . . .!

Marat (*cross*) If it's a practical joke . . .! It wasn't exactly easy to get here!

Lika Poor thing, you're tired . . .

Marat I suppose I am. – I had a strange dream on the plane. I was standing on a huge bridge. It was unfinished –

that is, I had to complete it. The wind was howling . . .
I looked about me and I saw both banks. On one bank
was my childhood, the May Day parades, the battleship
Marat, my father with his friends . . . On the other, the
post-war peace, the new life . . . But I'm standing in the
middle and the waves are getting bigger, the tide's getting
stronger, and I can't, I just can't join up the opposite
banks . . .

Lika (*softly*) What will be will be. (*suddenly astonished*)
Oh my God, what will be will be!

Marat What are you on about?

Lika You left, and I thought everything was fine between
Leonidik and me. I gave my word, didn't I? And now
here we are three weeks later . . . and the rules have
changed . . .

Leonidik returns, carrying a package.

Leonidik (*finger to his lips*) Sssh . . . only me . . . (*He
goes to the table and pours himself some wine.*) Now I'm
going to have a drink. No, Lika, don't start – I'm going
to have a drink. (*Raises his glass.*) My health! – what's
left of it. (*Drinks.*) Not bad at all, that.

*He unwraps the package and hands Lika a bouquet of
flowers.*

These are for you. Quite hard to procure, but he managed.

Lika Thank you, but –

Leonidik What am I going to say? – We've been together
for thirteen years and I love you now as I loved you
on the very first day. But I love you in my own peculiar
way. No less, but no more. Anyway that's not the issue. –
I simply haven't justified your hopes. You put a lot into
me. You neglected yourself. But all for nothing.

Lika Do I have to believe that?

Leonidik I must be alone. If I don't do it now I never will. You know me, Lika – I'm weak.

Lika (*desperate*) Marat, speak to him! Tell him that –

Marat No. I shan't.

Leonidik My train leaves at ten minutes to one. I'll have a nice long sabbatical. (*Pause.*) I am an individualist. You've said so yourself. And I need to be alone. (*to Marat*) You have nothing to fear. You're stronger. And the pair of you can't live without each other, that's transparently obvious. I'm right, aren't I? Do not lie.

Marat is silent.

Please – don't be a real man.

Marat . . . You're right.

Leonidik (*affectionately*) Lika . . .?

Lika Goodbye.

Leonidik Full marks! You both understand! Fair enough, I knew you would. Marat, you said that on the brink of death it isn't too late to start over. You were being melodramatic, as usual. But you got me thinking . . .

The clock strikes twelve times.

It's the New Year.

They all go to the table and Lika pours wine.

(*Raising his glass, softly*) We must never betray the winter of '42.

Marat (*raising his glass*) We must never come down to earth. (*to Lika*) Promise?

Lika (*raising her glass, whispers*) I promise you both.

They drink the toast.

Leonidik Well, I better be off. He packed his suitcase earlier. It's next door. This man has foresight. We'll see each other again, won't we?

Marat . . . You're trying to tell me that I'm more of a coward than you are.

Leonidik In a sense. (*to Lika*) Perhaps because he loves you more than I do. (*Kisses her hand.*) Who knows? (*He stops at the door.*) But there will always be a bit of me here, in this room. (*He takes a fork and tries his salad.*) Stupendous. (*Pours another glass of wine and drinks.*) And that was his last glass of wine. If I can give you up – why, I can give that up too! (*He stares at the two of them.*) Till we meet again.

Leonidik exits. Lika stares at the food on the table. Marat lights a cigarette with trembling hands. His voice is unsteady.

Marat On the first of May, 1945, we fought our way into the courtyard of a toy factory in Breslau. We were bombarded by mortar fire. There were seven of us. Only I survived.

Lika . . . Why tell me this?

Marat Because I can't get out of my mind the thought that I might have died, that day . . . and this moment, this very moment, would never have been.

Lika Marat . . .

Marat Yes . . .?

Lika He's all on his own . . . out there on the empty street . . .

Marat No, don't, just don't pity him, do you hear me? Don't. For him everything starts afresh today. You must

87

believe in him, Lika! (*Pause. Nervously*) How's it going to be, us living together?

He falls silent, a little afraid, which Lika understands.

Lika Everything's going to be fine. (*softly*) The sixties . . . I believe in the sixties. They will bring happiness.

Marat They can't fail! We have such hopes!

Lika Just don't be afraid, don't be afraid to be happy! Don't be afraid, my poor hero.

The End.